Marine Mammals

by J.R. Hilt

Contents

Introduction	2
Whales	4
Dolphins	6
Sea Lions	8
Sea Otters	10

Pioneer Valley Educational Press, Inc.

INTRODUCTION

Marine **mammals** live in the sea.
They are like humans,
dogs, cats, elephants, and other mammals.
They breathe air.
Most marine mammals have thick layers
of **blubber** that keep their bodies
warm in the water.
Marine mammals usually give birth to only one
baby at a time.

In this book, you will read about some of the marine mammals: whales, dolphins, sea lions, and sea otters.

WHALES

The blue whale is the largest living animal on Earth. All whales are very large animals. The body of the whale is long and round in the middle.

A whale has **flippers** on the front of its body. It has two fins on the tail called **flukes**. It swims by moving its tail up and down.

The whale can stay underwater for a long time. It must come to the surface of the water to breathe air. The whale breathes through a **blowhole** on top of its head.

DOLPHINS

Dolphins are fast swimmers. They use their tail fin, called a fluke, to move quickly through the water.

Dolphins are very smart. Dolphins live together in schools that are called pods.
They talk to each other by making whistles and clicking sounds. Dolphin clicks can be heard from very far away.

Dolphins like to jump and play. They can be seen playing with seaweed or play-fighting with other dolphins. They also like to ride waves.

SEA LIONS

Sea lions have flippers to help them swim. A sea lion has a small earflap on each side of its head. Sea lions can turn their back flippers forward to help them walk on land.

Sea lions make a roaring noise. That is how they got their name. They can also honk and bark. A baby sea lion is called a pup. A pup can find its mother just by the sound she makes.

Sea lions are very clever mammals. Sometimes they do tricks in shows at zoos, marine parks, and circuses.

SEA OTTERS

Sea otters love to float on their backs on the water. They sleep and eat this way, too. Sea otters will place a shellfish and a flat rock on their chests while floating. They smash the shellfish against the rock until it breaks open. Now they have a tasty meal.

Sea otters do not have blubber. They have thick fur that keeps them warm in chilly water.

Baby sea otters are called pups. Mother sea otters feed their pups milk and quickly teach them to swim and hunt.

flipper: A wide, flat limb that helps sea animals swim

fluke: either half of the triangular tail of a marine mammal

blowhole: nostrils at the top of the head used for breathing

mammals: animals that make milk to feed babies, are warm blooded, and have hair-covered skin

blubber: the fat layer between the skin and muscle of whales and other marine mammals